# ROBERT SCHUMANN

## FANTASY PIECES, OP. 73
## THREE ROMANCES, OP. 94

Jerome Bunke, *Clarinet*
Hidemitsu Hayashi, *Piano*

## CONTENTS

| TITLE | B♭ CLARINET | A CLARINET |
|---|---|---|
| Fantasy No.1 | 2 | 12 |
| Fantasy No. 2 | 4 | 14 |
| Fantasy No. 3 | 6 | 16 |
| | | |
| Romance No. 1 | 8 | 18 |
| Romance No. 2 | 9 | 19 |
| Romance No. 3 | 10 | 20 |

To access audio visit:
www.halleonard.com/mylibrary

Enter Code
5400-3112-5587-6789

T0078546

ISBN 978-1-59615-237-3

**Music Minus One**

EXCLUSIVELY DISTRIBUTED BY

**HAL•LEONARD®**
7777 W. BLUEMOUND RD. P.O. BOX 13819 MILWAUKEE, WI 53213

Visit Hal Leonard Online at
www.halleonard.com

# fantasy pieces

## 1

CLARINET IN B FLAT

**Zart und mit Ausdruck**
Tenderly and expressively

# 2

**CLARINET IN B FLAT**

**Lebhaft leicht**
**Lively and lightly**

CODA

Nach und nach ruhiger    More and more calmly

# 3

**CLARINET IN B FLAT**

5 taps precede music

**Rasch und mit Feuer** Quickly, with fire

# 3 romances

## 1

**CLARINET IN B FLAT**

# 2

4 taps precede music

**Einfach, innig  Semplice, affettuoso**

un poco piu mosso

a tempo

# 3

**CLARINET IN B FLAT**

# Clarinet in A

# *fantasy pieces*

## 1

**CLARINET IN A**

**Zart und mit Ausdruck**
**Tenderly and expressively**

# 2

## CLARINET IN A

**Lebhaft leicht**
**Lively and lightly**

### Coda
**Nach und nach ruhiger** More and more calmly

# 3

**CLARINET IN A**

**Rasch und mit Feuer**
Quickly with fire

5 taps precede music

# 3 romances

## 1

**Not fast**
**Nicht schnell**

**CLARINET IN A**

# 2

**CLARINET IN A**

4 taps precede music.

**Einfach, innig  Semplice, affettuoso**

**Etwas lebhafter**
Poco vivo

# 3

**CLARINET IN A**